iMath
Readers

Toy Tally:
How Many Toys Are There?

by Donna Loughran

Content Consultant
David T. Hughes
Mathematics Curriculum Specialist

NORWOOD HOUSE PRESS
Chicago, IL

Norwood House Press
PO Box 316598
Chicago, IL 60631

For information regarding Norwood House Press, please visit our website at
www.norwoodhousepress.com or call 866-565-2900.

Special thanks to: Heidi Doyle
Production Management: Six Red Marbles
Editors: Linda Bullock and Kendra Muntz
Printed in Heshan City, Guangdong, China. 208N—012013

Paperback ISBN: 978-1-60357-492-1

The Library of Congress has cataloged the original hardcover edition with the following
call number: 2012034230

CONTENTS

Note to Caregivers:

Throughout this book, many questions are posed to the reader. Some are open-ended and ask what the reader thinks. Discuss these questions with your child and guide him or her in thinking through the possible answers and outcomes. There are also questions posed which have a specific answer. Encourage your child to read through the text to determine the correct answer. Most importantly, encourage answers grounded in reality while also allowing imaginations to soar. Information to help support you as you share the book with your child is provided in the back in the **Additional Notes** section.

Bold words are defined in the glossary in the back of the book.

A New Playroom

Mona's mother is a doctor. She works at a children's **hospital**. A hospital is a place where sick children and adults receive care. The children's hospital wants to make a new playroom.

"We have lots of old toys," Mona said. "We could take those to the hospital."

"Yes," said her mother. "But, we also need some money because we want to paint the room."

Mona shouted, "I have an idea! We can have a toy **sale**. We can sell our toys. We can ask our friends to help. Then, we will give the money we make to the hospital."

Dr. Singer smiled. "That is a wonderful idea. You will make the children at the hospital very happy."

iMath Ideas: Toy Tally

Mona's friends brought lots of toys. She needed a way to keep track of them. Mona had some ideas about how to do this.

Idea 1: Make a Tally Table.
Mona made a **tally table**. She made one **tally mark** for each toy. For the fifth tally, she drew a slanted line across the first four tally marks. That made a set of five marks. This made counting easier.

Next, she counted the tally marks. She wrote the numbers in the table.

Toys	Tally	Number
Teddy bears	|||	3
Cars			1
Balls	|||||	5

Do you think a tally table is a good way to know what toys are for sale?

Idea 2: Make a Picture Graph. A **picture graph** uses pictures to show numbers. Mona drew one picture of every toy. Then, she put the pictures in a graph so she could see how many she had.

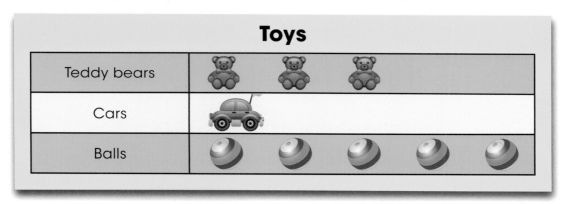

Idea 3: Make a Bar Graph. Next, Mona made a **bar graph**. A bar graph uses bars to show numbers.

Do you think a picture graph or a bar graph is a good way to know what toys are for sale?

Which do you like best: a tally table, a picture graph, or a bar graph? Why?

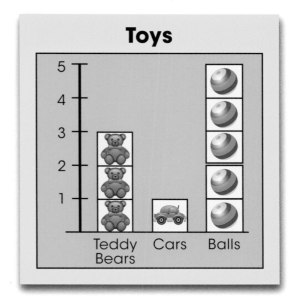

Discover Activity

Materials
- paper
- pencil
- toys

Make a Tally Table

Gather some of your toys.
Put them together in groups.
For example, put soft toys, like teddy bears, in one group. Put hard toys, like cars and trains, in another group.

Draw a tally table. Write the names of the toys in the chart. Then, make one tally mark for each toy in each group. Count the tally marks and write the numbers.

Next, use your tally table to make a graph.
You can make a picture graph or a bar graph.

Share your graph with an adult. Can you think about some ways that graphs can help you?

Tallying the Toys

"Wow! Your friends are very kind," Dr. Singer said. "I did not think they would give away so many toys."

"It's wonderful!" said Mona. "Look at this. I made a tally table to show what toys came today."

Toys	Tally	Number	Name
Music toys	||	2	Two
Boats	|	1	One
Space toys	∦|	5	Five

How many boats are there?

How many more space toys than boats are there?

The next day, Mona's friend, Jacob, visited.
"I thought you might want this train," he said.
"I don't play with it very often. Maybe another child would like it."

"That is a fun train!" said Mona. She put it with the other toys. Then, she and Jacob made a picture graph to show more new toys that had come that day.

Toys

Trains	
Pull toys	
Rockets	

How many pull toys did her friends bring this day?

How many more rockets are there than trains?

Later, Mona's friend, Lily, came over. She brought lots of **action toys**. Some were action toys of people and some were of animals.

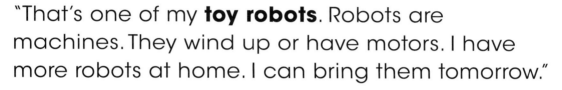

Mona pointed to a toy dog. The dog had a red cape. "What is that?" she asked.

"That's one of my **toy robots**. Robots are machines. They wind up or have motors. I have more robots at home. I can bring them tomorrow."

Mona smiled and said, "Great! Thank you."

They made a bar graph to show the action toys.

How many action toys are people?

How many more people toys are there than animal toys?

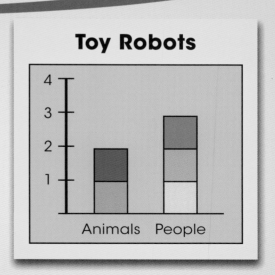

Toy Robots

The next day was a big toy day! Maria, Lucy, and Scott came. Their arms were full of soft toys.

"I have too many toys," Maria said. "I kept them on my bed and there was never any room for me! But, now I have lots of room!"

Mona laughed. Her friends helped her carry all of the toys inside.

Together, they made a tally table to show the soft toys.

Soft Toys	Tally	Number	Name
African animals	‖‖‖ ‖‖	8	Eight
Sea animals	‖‖‖ ‖	?	?
Birds	‖‖‖	4	Four

How many sea animals are there in all?

How many more African animals are there than birds?

Mona looked at her own toys. She has lots of wind-up toys. Sometimes, she winds them all up at the same time. It is fun to watch them go in all directions.

Her favorite toys are small birds. They used to belong to her grandmother. So, they are very special.

Mona made a picture graph to show how many wind-up toys she has in all.

Wind-Up Toys

How many wind-up animal toys does Mona have?

How many more wind-up cars does she have than toy robots?

Math at Work

Some teddy bear makers use furry cloth to make bears. But there are things to do before they cut the cloth. They draw pictures of the bear. They also make paper patterns.

A **paper pattern** is a flat drawing. It has all of the pieces that will fit together to make a bear. Before they draw paper patterns, teddy bear makers take measurements. How tall will the bear be? How round will it be? Will it have large ears? Will it have a long nose? Every piece must be the right size.

Teddy bear makers cut out the pattern pieces. They lay them on the furry cloth. They cut around the patterns and sew the pieces of cloth together. They fill their bears with stuffing. Then, they add eyes, a nose, and a mouth to finish the bear. This is how new teddy bears are born!

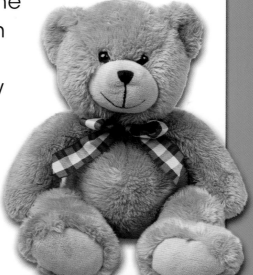

What's the Word?

Teddy Bear is a nursery rhyme. You can read or sing the rhyme.

Teddy bear, Teddy bear,
Touch the ground.
Teddy bear, Teddy bear,
Turn around.
Teddy bear, Teddy bear,
Show your shoe.
Teddy bear, Teddy bear,
That will do.

Teddy bear, Teddy bear,
Run upstairs.
Teddy bear, Teddy bear,
Say your prayers.
Teddy bear, Teddy bear,
Blow out the light.
Teddy bear, Teddy bear,
Say good night.

Has anyone read this rhyme to you before? Will you read it to your teddy bear or another toy tonight?

Connecting to Science

Many ships cross the oceans. They carry things from one place to another. Often, the things they carry are in large boxes. The boxes are made of metal or wood.

In 1991, a ship left Hong Kong. It sailed across the Pacific Ocean. It was on its way to the United States.

The ship held a huge box of rubber ducks. The box fell off the ship. It broke open. The rubber ducks floated away.

Rivers of water move through an ocean. The river in the part of the ocean where the box fell moves in a circle. Some of the rubber ducks were caught in the circle of water. But other ducks got away. Ocean water carried them toward land. The rubber ducks landed on beaches, where people found them.

Scientists asked these people to tell them when and where they had found the ducks. This information helped the scientists find the paths the ducks had taken and helped them understand how water in the ocean moves.

More Toys!

The day of the yard sale was coming. Mona and her friends collected more toys.

"Look what I have," said Kaitlin. Kaitlin stood at Mona's door. Her parents were with her.

"My parents called their friends. They all sent toys to our house. So, here are all of the toys! We have more boxes in the car!"

The word "donation" is on the box. A donation is something that a person gives to someone else. Mona and her friends collected toy donations.

Mona's mom was with her. They both smiled big smiles. "Thank you so much," Dr. Singer said. "Please, come in. And bring the toys!"

Mona wanted to know what kinds of and how many toys she had for the sale.

Idea 1: Make a Tally Table. Mona could make a **tally table**. She could make one tally mark for each toy. Then, she could count the tallies and write the numbers.

Idea 2: Make a Picture Graph. Mona could make a **picture graph**. She could draw one picture for each toy. This would work. But it would take a long time to draw the pictures.

Idea 3: Make a Bar Graph. Mona could make a **bar graph**. But she would have to count all of the toys first. Making a bar graph would take more time.

Mona decided to make this tally table.

Toys	Tally	Number
Soft toys	ⅢⅠ ΙΙΙΙ	9
Dolls	ⅢⅠ Ι	6
Cars and Trucks	ⅢⅠ ⅢⅠ ΙΙ	?
Balls	ⅢⅠ ⅢⅠ	?
Musical toys	ΙΙΙΙ	4

How many cars and trucks did Kaitlin's family bring?

How many balls did they bring?

People came from miles around to buy toys. Mona collected more than $100! This was enough money to paint the hospital's new playroom.

There were toys left over, too. Mona's mother put them in the playroom. Now, sick children will have a fun and safe place to play!

What Comes Next?

Look around your house. Make a list of objects you can count. You count blocks, dolls, or rocks. What are some other things you can count?

Put the objects you choose into groups. For example, say you have lots of books. Put the animal books in one group. Put fairy tale books in another group. Keep going until you have grouped all of the books.

Then, make a tally table. List the groups that you made. Make a tally mark for each thing in each group. Next, count the tally marks. Write the numbers in the tally table.

Share your tally table with friends or an adult. Explain what the numbers in your tally table mean.

GLOSSARY

action toys: people or animal figures that have parts that move.

bar graph: a graph that uses bars to show how many things there are.

hospital: a place where doctors and nurses take care of sick children and adults.

paper pattern: a flat drawing used to cut out a design.

picture graph: a graph that uses pictures to show how many things there are.

sale: a place or event where items are bought with money.

tally mark: a straight mark that stands for one thing.

tally table: a chart that uses straight marks to show how many things there are.

toy robot: a toy that winds up or has a motor.

FURTHER READING

FICTION
The Great Graph Contest, by Loreen Leedy, Holiday House, 2006

NONFICTION
Graphing the School Cleanup, by Suzanne Barchers, Capstone Press, 2011
Let's Make a Bar Graph, by Robin Nelson, Lerner Publishing Group, 2012

Additional Notes

The page references below provide answers to questions asked throughout the book. Questions whose answers will vary are not addressed.

Page 9: There is one (1) boat. There are four more space toys than there are boats. $5 - 1 = 4$.

Page 10: There are five (5) pull toys. There are three more rockets than there are trains. $4 - 1 = 3$.

Page 11: Three (3) action toys are people. There is one more people toy than there are animal toys. $3 - 2 = 1$.

Page 12: There are six (6) sea animals. There are four more African animals than there are birds. $8 - 4 = 4$.

Page 13: Mona has eight (8) wind-up animals. She has three more cars than she has robots. $5 - 2 = 3$.

Page 20: There are twelve (12) cars and trucks. There are ten (10) balls.

INDEX

Content Consultant

David T. Hughes

David is an experienced mathematics teacher, writer, presenter, and adviser. He serves as a consultant for the Partnership for Assessment of Readiness for College and Careers. David has also worked as the Senior Program Coordinator for the Charles A. Dana Center at The University of Texas at Austin and was an editor and contributor for the *Mathematics Standards in the Classroom* series.